KU-081-391

WITHDRAWN FROM STOCK

Limerick City Library

3 0002 50049418 2

burgers
& sliders

burgers & sliders

Miranda Ballard *of* **Muddy Boots**

photography by **Clare Winfield**

LONDON · NEW YORK

This book is dedicated to Roland.

Senior Designer Iona Hoyle

Editor Ellen Parnavelas

Production Co-ordinator Gary Hayes

Art Director Leslie Harrington

Editorial Director Julia Charles

Prop Stylist Iris Bromet

Food styling Maud Eden

Indexer Hilary Bird

First published in 2013 by
Ryland Peters & Small
20–21 Jockey's Fields
London WC1R 4BW
and
519 Broadway, 5th Floor
New York, NY 10012

www.rylandpeters.com

10 9 8 7 6 5 4 3 2 1

Text © Miranda Ballard 2013
Design and photographs
© Ryland Peters & Small 2013

Printed in China

The author's moral rights have been asserted.
All rights reserved. No part of this publication
may be reproduced, stored in a retrieval system
or transmitted in any form or by any means,
electronic, mechanical, photocopying or
otherwise, without the prior permission of
the publisher.

UK ISBN: 978-1-84975-364-7
US ISBN: 978-1-84975-422-4

CIP records for this book are available from
the British Library and the US Library of Congress.

Notes

• All spoon measurements are level unless otherwise specified.

• Ovens should be preheated to the specified temperatures. All ovens work slightly differently. We recommend using an oven thermometer and suggest you consult the maker's handbook for any special instructions, particularly if you are cooking in a fan-assisted/convection oven, as you will need to adjust temperatures according to manufacturer's instructions.

• Eggs are large (UK) and extra large (US) unless otherwise specified. Uncooked or partially cooked eggs should not be served to the very old, frail, young children, pregnant women or those with compromised immune systems.

• When the recipe calls for the grated zest of citrus fruit, buy unwaxed fruit and wash well before using. If you can only find treated fruit, scrub well in warm, soapy water and rinse before using.

Author's acknowledgements

To my family and in-laws for being happy to taste up to 14 burgers in one sitting. To such amazing publishers who would give a new girl a try. And to my husband Roland, who is the source of every smile and inspiration.

D 11022

CITY OF LIMERICK PUBLIC LIBRARY

641/s

contents

the muddy boots story

A few years ago, my husband Roland and I were having great fun living in London, working in film and television and not imagining for a moment that we'd be running our own company. However, we believed that there was a market for quality burgers that promoted using top cuts of the finest and most ethically farmed beef and so Muddy Boots was born. Fortunately, some supermarkets agreed and, three years later, our products are already stocked in over 200 stores across the country.

We are now even more passionate about making burgers than when we started our business and we love inventing new interpretations of the classic burger. When our friends and family come over, they know that they can always expect to find a delicious burger served with homemade trimmings waiting for them on the table – and we know they have enjoyed helping us develop all of our new and exciting recipes.

On special occasions, we might serve up the gourmet Beef Wellington Burger, flavoured with mushrooms, shallots and mustard and served between two rounds of meltingly flaky pastry. The Mexican Burger topped with sour cream, fresh tomato salsa and guacamole is perfect for a lunchtime fiesta with friends and family. Our party guests are always delighted with the light and fresh Chicken Caesar Sliders, and the Pork and Apple Sliders are a particular favourite with the little ones.

Muddy Boots is still growing and we have a long way to go but we've never looked back. We hope the recipes in this, our first book, will inspire you to enjoy making your own burgers just as much as we do!

making, shaping & cooking

There's a reason that burgers have become associated with fast food, and that is because they are so easy to make and simple to cook. This has never meant that the ingredients need to be poor quality, but the time it takes to make burgers – even from scratch – is very quick.

After selecting good-quality meat and other ingredients, the rest is very simple.
My top tips for making the perfect burger are:

1. *Get stuck in.* Put the ingredients in a bowl and work the them together with your hands. This will ensure that the ingredients are mixed together properly, as well as binding the mixture together much better than you would be able to using a food processor.

2. *Squeeze.* There are ingredients such as egg and breadcrumbs in these recipes, where needed, to help bind the mixture together. However, the best binding is achieved by squeezing the burgers with your hands before cooking. Really clench the ingredients together and then flatten into a patty shape – the tighter the better. It won't make the texture of the burger less fluffy. It's only the quality of the meat that dictates that.

3. *Oven, fry or grill?* If there are a lot of chunky ingredients in the mixture, like there are in the Beef, Goat Cheese and Bean Burger, you're going to be safer to oven-cook the burger to make sure it keeps its form. Simpler burger mixtures that bind together more easily, such as the Classic Beef Burger, are better fried or grilled/broiled.

4. *What size?* The good thing about making burgers yourself is that you can make them any size you like. I tend to make 160-g/6-oz burgers for my husband and 120-g/4-oz burgers for myself. You can make the burgers different weights – just remember to allow a little extra cooking time for the bigger ones.

Why go to a restaurant when you can make these delicious gourmet burgers at home? This easy recipe combines a tasty beef patty with all the trimmings. Serve with Classic Homecut Fries for the ultimate burger experience.

ultimate restaurant burger
with bacon, cheese & tomato relish

For the tomato relish

1 tablespoon olive oil

1 onion, sliced

1 garlic clove, crushed

1 fresh red chilli/chile, chopped

800 g/3½ cups canned chopped tomatoes

200 ml/¾ cup red wine vinegar

200 g/1 cup sugar

30 g/3 tablespoons capers, rinsed

3 or 4 baby gherkins, chopped

a handful of fresh coriander/cilantro

sea salt and freshly ground black pepper

For the burgers

340 g/12 oz. lean minced/ground beef

1 tablespoon olive or vegetable oil

a large pinch of sea salt and freshly ground black pepper

To serve

2 slices bacon

4 slices Cheddar cheese

2 large burger buns

butter, for spreading

2 tablespoons American mustard

2 pickled gherkins, thinly sliced

75 g/1 cup chopped lettuce

Classic Homecut Fries (page 57)

Makes 2 burgers

To make the tomato relish, heat the oil in a frying pan/skillet set over medium heat. Add the onion, garlic and chilli/chile and fry, stirring occasionally, until soft.

Add the tomatoes and mix well. Add the vinegar and sugar and bring to the boil. Reduce the heat and simmer for 30 minutes. Season with salt and pepper, to taste. The relish should be the consistency of jam. Stir in the capers and gherkins and the coriander/cilantro. Taste and adjust the seasoning, if necessary.

To make the burgers, put the beef in a bowl with the salt and pepper. Work together with your hands until evenly mixed. Divide the beef mixture in half and shape into two burger patties. Press each burger down to make them nice and flat.

Heat the oil in a frying pan and fry the burgers over medium–high heat for 5 minutes on each side until cooked through.

Meanwhile, heat a separate frying pan until hot and fry the bacon slices until crisp. Remove from the pan and set aside.

When the burgers are cooked, remove from the pan and top each with two slices of cheese. Set aside to allow the cheese to melt slightly.

Slice the burger buns in half and lightly toast them under the grill/broiler or in the toaster.

Spread butter on the cut sides of each bun. Squeeze a little mustard onto the base and put the cooked burgers on top. Add a generous spoonful of tomato relish to each and top with the bacon, gherkins and lettuce. Finish the burgers with the lids of the buns and serve with Classic Homecut Fries.

classic beef

*With all the flavours of Italy, this hearty and heavenly burger
will transport your tastebuds to an Italian lakeside table
adorned with Chianti and candlelight.*

Italian burger
with olives, sun-dried tomatoes & pesto

Preheat the grill/broiler to medium.

Put the beef in a bowl with the olives, sun-dried tomatoes, tomato purée/
paste, pesto and salt and pepper. Work together with your hands until evenly
mixed. Divide the beef mixture in half and shape into two burger patties. Press
each burger down to make them nice and flat.

Put the burgers on a baking sheet and grill/broil the burgers for 5 minutes on
each side until cooked through. Remove from the grill/broiler and set aside.
Leave the grill/broiler on.

Slice the ciabatta rolls in half and lightly toast them under the hot grill/broiler.

Put a cooked burger on the bottom half of each ciabatta roll and top with a
large spoonful of pesto mayo. Finish the burgers with the lids of the ciabatta
rolls and serve with a bowl of olives on the side, if liked.

For the burgers

220 g/8 oz. lean minced/ground
beef

4 pitted black olives, finely
chopped

2 sun-dried tomatoes, finely
chopped

2 teaspoons tomato purée/paste

2 teaspoons pesto

a pinch of sea salt and freshly
ground black pepper

To serve

2 ciabatta rolls

Pesto Mayo (page 59)

a bowl of black olives (optional)

Makes 2 burgers

Sometimes less is more and a simple burger made with good-quality beef speaks for itself. It's worth making a batch of our Homemade Tomato Ketchup to serve with these burgers – it is so much tastier than any store-bought variety.

classic beef burger
with tomato ketchup & lettuce

For the burgers

220 g/8 oz. lean minced/ground beef

2 teaspoons tomato purée/paste

1½ tablespoons fresh breadcrumbs

1 teaspoon chopped fresh parsley

1 tablespoon olive or vegetable oil

a large pinch of sea salt and freshly ground black pepper

To serve

2 sesame seeded burger buns

Homemade Tomato Ketchup (page 61)

a few lettuce leaves

Classic Homecut Fries (page 57)

Makes 2 burgers

Put the beef in a bowl with the tomato purée/paste, breadcrumbs, parsley and salt and pepper. Work together with your hands until evenly mixed. Divide the beef mixture in half and shape into two burger patties. Press each burger down to make them nice and flat.

Heat the oil in a frying pan/skillet and fry the burgers over medium-high heat for 5 minutes on each side until cooked through.

Slice the burger buns in half. Spread a spoonful of Homemade Tomato Ketchup on the base of each bun and put the cooked burgers on top. Put a few lettuce leaves on top of each burger and finish with the lids of the buns. Serve with Classic Homecut Fries.

Eating beans straight out of the pods when I was young is a fond memory of mine. I still do it now that we grow them but I always make sure I save some for these summertime burgers.

beef, goat cheese & bean burger
with pesto mayo

Preheat the oven to 180°C (350°F) Gas 4.

Melt the butter in a frying pan/skillet set over medium heat and add the garlic. Add the broad/fava beans and stir until browned. When cooked, remove from the pan, crush with a fork and set aside to cool.

Put the beef in a bowl with the goat cheese, tomato purée/paste, egg, breadcrumbs and salt and pepper. Work together with your hands until evenly mixed. Add the crushed broad/fava beans and mix again. Divide the mixture in half and shape into two burger patties. Press each burger down to make them nice and flat. Lay the burgers on a baking sheet and bake in the oven for 20 minutes, turning halfway through cooking.

Slice the bread rolls in half and spread both cut sides of each roll with a little butter. Put a cooked burger on the bottom half of each bread roll and top with a spoonful of pesto mayo. Finish the burgers with the lids of the bread rolls and serve with a watercress and radish salad, if liked.

For the burgers

15 g/1 tablespoon butter

1 garlic clove, finely chopped

30 g/¼ cup shelled fresh broad/fava beans

160 g/6 oz. lean minced/ground beef

15 g/½ oz. goat cheese, crumbled

4 teaspoons tomato purée/paste

1 tablespoon beaten egg

3 tablespoons fresh breadcrumbs

a pinch of sea salt and freshly ground black pepper

To serve

2 wholemeal/wholewheat bread rolls

butter, for spreading

Pesto Mayo (page 59)

watercress and radish salad (optional)

Makes 2 burgers

*This hearty recipe is the burger interpretation of a traditional
chili con carne. These deliciously spicy burgers are just as good
served on open bread rolls or simply as they are.*

chili con carne burger
wrapped in grilled courgette slices

For the burgers

1 tablespoon olive oil

1 large courgette/zucchini, sliced
lengthways into thin strips

200 g/7 oz. lean minced/ground
beef

2 tablespoons chopped cooked
kidney beans

4 teaspoons tomato purée/paste

½ red onion, finely chopped

3 tablespoons fresh breadcrumbs

1 tablespoon beaten egg

1 fresh red chilli/chile, finely
chopped

a pinch of ground cumin

sea salt and freshly ground black
pepper

To serve

4 slices Cheddar cheese

2 wholemeal/wholewheat bread
rolls (optional)

2 tablespoons sour cream

Classic Homecut Fries (page 57)

Makes 2 burgers

Preheat the grill/broiler to medium.

Heat the oil in a ridged stovetop grill pan/griddle. Add the
courgette/zucchini slices and cook over high heat, turning
occasionally, until browned on each side. Set aside to cool.

Put the beef in a bowl with the kidney beans, tomato purée/paste,
onion, breadcrumbs, egg, chilli/chile, cumin and salt and pepper.
Work together with your hands until evenly mixed. Divide the beef
mixture in half and shape into two burger patties. Squeeze them
together to keep the ingredients well packed inside then press each
burger down to make them nice and flat.

Put the burgers on a baking sheet and grill/broil for 5 minutes on
each side until cooked through. When the burgers are cooked,
remove from the grill/broiler and top each with two cheese slices.
Wrap a slice of grilled/broiled courgette/zucchini around each
burger and then fold the slices of courgette/zucchini over the top so
they meet in the middle.

Slice the bread rolls in half, if using, and put a wrapped burger on
the bottom half of each bread roll. Serve with with sour cream for
spooning and Classic Homecut Fries on the side.

A full-on Mexican feast, this burger contains all the fiesty flavours of Mexico as well as the accompaniments, so they power through with every bite. If you like it hot, just add some extra chilli/chile.

Mexican burger
with sour cream, fresh tomato salsa & guacamole

To make the Guacamole, put the avocado in a bowl with the chilli/chile, lime juice, coriander/cilantro and salt and pepper, to taste. Mash together with a fork.

To make the Fresh Tomato Salsa, put the tomatoes in a bowl with the onion and chillies/chiles. Add the lime juice and mix well, then add the sugar and season with salt. Stir in the coriander/cilantro.

To make the burgers, put the beef in a bowl with the breadcrumbs, onion, tomato purée/paste, cheese, lime zest, chilli/chile, egg and salt and pepper. Work together with your hands until evenly mixed. Divide the beef mixture in half and shape into two burger patties. Press each burger down to make them nice and flat.

Heat the oil in a frying pan/skillet and fry the burgers over medium–high heat for 5 minutes on each side until cooked through.

Preheat the grill/broiler to medium. Splash a few drops of water on each tortilla and lay them under the grill/broiler for a few seconds on each side to lightly toast. Spread both tortillas with sour cream and put a cooked burger on top of each. Top with a spoonful each of Guacamole and Fresh Tomato Salsa. Sprinkle with coriander/cilantro and serve, folding the sides of the tortilla around the burger to eat.

For the guacamole

1 large, ripe avocado, peeled and pitted

½ fresh red chilli/chile, finely chopped

1 teaspoon freshly squeezed lime juice

a handful of fresh coriander/cilantro

a pinch of sea salt and freshly ground black pepper

For the fresh tomato salsa

500 g/1 lb. ripe tomatoes, peeled and finely diced

½ a red onion, finely chopped

1–2 small green chillies/chiles, deseeded and finely chopped

3 tablespoons freshly squeezed lime juice

a pinch of sugar

2 tablespoons finely chopped fresh coriander/cilantro

sea salt

For the burgers

180 g/6 oz. lean minced/ground beef

3 tablespoons breadcrumbs

½ red onion, finely chopped

2 teaspoons tomato purée/paste

20 g/3 tablespoons grated Monteray Jack or sharp Cheddar cheese

freshly grated zest of ½ a lime

½ a fresh red chilli/chile, finely chopped

1 tablespoon beaten egg

1 tablespoon olive or vegetable oil

a pinch of sea salt and freshly ground black pepper

To serve

sour cream

2 large flour tortillas

a handful of fresh coriander/cilantro, chopped

Makes 2 burgers

Light, bright and tangy, this unusual combination of ingredients works together to create a delicious summertime burger. For a lighter option, serve this burger without a bun on a bed of chopped lamb's lettuce.

beef, roasted red pepper & lime burger
with crème fraîche & lamb's lettuce

For the burgers

½ red (bell) pepper, deseeded and chopped

2 tablespoons olive oil

200 g/7 oz. lean minced/ground beef

2 teaspoons paprika

freshly grated zest of ½ a lime

3 tablespoons fresh breadcrumbs

1 tablespoon beaten egg

1 garlic clove, finely chopped

a pinch of sea salt and freshly ground black pepper

To serve

2 seeded wholemeal/wholewheat bread rolls (optional)

a handful of lamb's lettuce/corn salad leaves, chopped

crème fraîche/sour cream

lime wedges, for squeezing

Makes 2 burgers

Preheat the grill/broiler to high.

Drizzle the pepper pieces with the oil and sprinkle with salt and pepper. Put them on a baking sheet and cook under the grill/broiler for 8–10 minutes, shaking regularly to brown evenly. Remove from the grill/broiler and set aside to cool.

Put the beef in a bowl with the paprika, lime zest, breadcrumbs, egg, garlic and salt and pepper. Add the roasted pepper pieces and work together with your hands until evenly mixed. Divide the beef mixture in half and shape into two burger patties. Press each burger down to make them nice and flat.

Put the burgers on a baking sheet and grill/broil for 5 minutes on each side until cooked through.

Slice the bread rolls in half, if using, and put a few lamb's lettuce/corn salad leaves on the bottom half of each bread roll. Add the cooked burgers and top with a large spoonful of crème fraîche/sour cream. Finish the burgers with the lids of the bread rolls, if using, and serve with lime wedges, for squeezing.

One of the fanciest of beef dishes, beef wellington also works wonderfully in a burger form! To create this gourmet delight, we have used pastry rounds instead of a bun and flavoured the delicious burgers with mustard, mushrooms and shallots.

beef wellington burger
in a shortcrust pastry 'bun'

Preheat the oven to 180°C (350°F) Gas 4.

To make the pastry, put the butter, flour and salt in a mixing bowl and rub together with your fingertips until it has the texture of breadcrumbs. Add 3 tablespoons of warm water and mix together. Add 3 more tablespoons of water and mix again. If the pastry feels too dry, add a drop more water to bind but not too much. It should not feel sticky. Wrap the pastry in clingfilm/plastic wrap and chill it in the fridge while you make the burgers.

Heat half the oil in a frying pan/skillet set over medium–high heat. Add the garlic, shallots and mushrooms and fry until soft and brown. Remove from the heat and add the wholegrain mustard, tomato purée/paste and thyme and mix well. Set aside to cool.

Remove the pastry from the fridge and roll out to a thickness of 1-cm/ ½-inch on a lightly-floured surface. Stamp out four pastry rounds using the cookie cutter.

Put the pastry rounds on a greased baking sheet and brush them with a little milk. Bake in the preheated oven for 15–20 minutes, until golden brown.

To make the burgers, put the beef in a bowl with the salt and pepper. Work together with your hands until evenly mixed. Add the shallot and mushroom mixture and mix again. Divide the mixture in half and shape into two burger patties. Press each burger down to make them nice and flat.

Heat the remaining oil in a frying pan and fry the burgers over medium–high heat for 5–6 minutes on each side until cooked through.

When cooked, remove the pastry rounds from the oven and lay one face up on each serving plate. Top with the cooked burgers and a handful of lamb's lettuce leaves. Cover with the remaining pastry rounds and serve with peas and any tomato chutney of your choice on the side.

For the pastry rounds

50 g/3 tablespoons unsalted butter, chilled and cubed

120 g/1 scant cup plain/ all-purpose flour, plus extra for rolling out

a little milk, for brushing

a large pinch of sea salt

For the burgers

2 tablespoons olive oil

1 garlic clove, finely chopped

2 shallots, finely chopped

6 mushrooms, finely chopped

¾ teaspoon wholegrain mustard

2 teaspoons tomato purée/paste

1 sprig of fresh thyme, chopped

300 g/10 oz. lean minced/ ground beef

a large pinch of sea salt and freshly ground black pepper

To serve

a handful of lamb's lettuce/ corn salad leaves

cooked peas

tomato chutney of your choice

a rolling pin

a 9-cm/3½-inch round cookie cutter

Makes 2 large burgers

Burgers aren't usually associated with warming meals but this recipe proves that they really can be the ideal comfort food. Just roast them in a pan with lots of lovely winter vegetables.

beef, leek & mushroom burger
with roasted root vegetables & mustard mayo

1 leek, finely chopped plus
½ a leek, roughly chopped

10 mushrooms, finely chopped

2 sprigs of fresh thyme, chopped

5 tablespoons olive oil

1 medium potato, peeled and chopped

1 sweet potato, peeled and chopped

½ butternut squash, peeled and chopped

1 carrot, peeled and chopped

1 red onion, roughly chopped

2 garlic cloves, finely chopped

1 sprig of fresh rosemary, chopped

420 g/15 oz. lean minced/ground beef

1½ tablespoons fresh breadcrumbs

sea salt and freshly ground black pepper

To serve
Mustard Mayo (page 58)
mixed green vegetables of your choice, cooked (optional)

Makes 4 burgers

Preheat the oven to 180°C (350°F) Gas 4.

Put the finely-chopped leek and mushrooms in a baking dish. Add the thyme and season with salt and pepper. Pour 3 tablespoons of the olive oil over the top and bake in the oven for 15–20 minutes until soft and browned. When cooked, remove from the oven and set aside to cool. Leave the oven on.

Meanwhile, bring a large saucepan of water to the boil. Add the remaining ½ leek, potato, sweet potato, squash and carrot and boil for 5 minutes. Drain the vegetables and put them in a baking dish. Add the onion, garlic and rosemary and drizzle the remaining olive oil over the top. Mix to coat and bake in the oven for 20 minutes.

To make the burgers, put the beef in a bowl with the breadcrumbs and salt and pepper. Work together with your hands until evenly mixed. Add the leek and mushroom mixture and mix again. Divide the mixture into quarters and shape into four burger patties. Press each burger down to make them nice and flat. After 20 minutes, remove the baking dish from the oven and stir the vegetables to mix. Make small spaces between the vegetables and nestle the burgers in the gaps.

Return to the oven for 20–25 minutes, turning the burgers over halfway through cooking. Put a spoonful of Mustard Mayo on top of each burger and top each with two cooked green beans, if liked. Serve with mixed green vegetables of your choice.

These simple beef sliders have a delightfully gooey mozzarella surprise in the middle – great for a party or as part of a buffet.

beef & mozzarella pearl sliders
with pesto mayo and rocket

Preheat the oven to 180°C (350°F) Gas 4.

Put the beef in a bowl with the tomato purée/paste, garlic and salt and pepper. Work together with your hands until evenly mixed. Divide the beef mixture into quarters and shape into four slider patties. Put a mozzarella pearl in the middle of each and then fold the beef mixture around it to reform the slider patties, with the mozzarella pearl hidden in the middle. Press each slider down to make them nice and flat.

Lay the sliders on a baking sheet and bake in the preheated oven for 20 minutes, turning halfway through cooking. When cooked, remove from the oven and let stand for 4 minutes before serving to allow the mozzarella to cool a little.

Slice the mini ciabattas in half and spread the bottom half of each with a little Pesto Mayo. Put a cooked slider on top and add a few rocket/arugula leaves. Finish the sliders with the lids of the mini ciabattas and serve.

For the sliders
200 g/7 oz. lean minced/ground beef

2 teaspoons tomato purée/paste

1 garlic clove, finely chopped

4 mozzarella pearls/bocconcini

a pinch of sea salt and freshly ground black pepper

To serve
4 mini ciabattas

Pesto Mayo (page 59)

a handful of rocket/arugula leaves

Makes 4 sliders

Capture the taste of South America wherever you are with these delicious beef sliders. Served with spicy Corn and Pepper Salsa and tangy Lime Mayo, these are guaranteed to create a fiesta of flavours for your tastebuds.

beef & black bean sliders
with corn & pepper salsa

For the Corn & Pepper Salsa

2 large corn cobs

3 tablespoons vegetable oil

4 spring onions/scallions, sliced

freshly squeezed juice of 1 lime

6 Pepperdew peppers, diced

2 tablespoons finely chopped coriander/cilantro

a dash of chilli/chili sauce

sea salt and freshly ground black pepper

For the sliders

1 tablespoon canned black beans

1 spring onion/scallion, sliced

1 garlic clove, finely chopped

2 teaspoons tomato purée/paste

a pinch of cayenne pepper

1 tablespoon chopped fresh coriander/cilantro

200 g/7 oz. lean minced/ground beef

40 g/3 tablespoons long grain rice, cooked and cooled

1 tablespoon olive or vegetable oil

a pinch of sea salt and freshly ground black pepper

To serve

4 mini poppyseed rolls

Lime Mayo (page 59)

Sweet Potato Fries (page 56)

Makes 4 sliders

To make the corn and pepper salsa, cut down the sides of the corn cobs with a sharp knife to remove the kernels. Heat 2 teaspoons of the oil in a frying pan/skillet set over medium heat. Add the corn and cook for 2–3 minutes until it begins to brown. Add the spring onions/scallions and cook for 1 minute. Transfer to a bowl and let cool.

Add the lime juice, peppers, coriander/cilantro and the remaining oil, and mix well. Add a dash of chilli/chili sauce and season with salt and pepper.

To make the sliders, blitz the black beans, spring onion/scallion, garlic, tomato purée/paste, cayenne pepper and and coriander/cilantro in a food processor. Pour the mixture into a mixing bowl, add the beef and work together with your hands until evenly mixed. Add the cooled rice, season with salt and pepper and mix again.

Divide the beef mixture into quarters and shape into four slider patties. Press each slider down to make them nice and flat.

Heat the oil in a frying pan and fry the sliders over medium–high heat for 4 minutes on each side until cooked through.

Slice the mini poppyseed rolls in half and spread the bottom half of each with Lime Mayo. Put a cooked slider on top of each and add a large spoonful of Corn and Pepper Salsa. Finish the sliders with the lids of the rolls and serve with Sweet Potato Fries on the side, if liked.

D 11022

These punchy Asian-style sliders are ideal for eating outdoors on a warm summer's evening. The lime and ginger soak perfectly into the meat and a touch of spice adds a welcome kick to every mouthful.

spicy beef & pork sliders
with ginger & lime

Put the beef and pork in a bowl with the chilli/chile, lime juice, ginger, breadcrumbs and salt and pepper. Work together with your hands until evenly mixed. Divide the beef mixture into six equal pieces and shape into six slider patties. Press each slider down to make them nice and flat.

Heat the oil in a frying pan/skillet and fry the sliders over medium–high heat for 3 minutes on each side until cooked through.

Put the chicory/Belgian endive leaves face up on a serving plate. Put a slider on top of each leaf, top with chilli/chile and spring onions/scallions. Put a cocktail stick/toothpick through the middle of each slider to hold them together, if liked, and serve.

For the sliders

100 g/3½ oz. lean minced/ground beef

100 g/3½ oz. lean minced/ground pork

1 fresh red or green chilli/chile, finely chopped

½ teaspoon ground ginger

1 tablespoon freshly squeezed lime juice

3 tablespoons fresh breadcrumbs

1 tablespoon olive or vegetable oil

a pinch of sea salt and freshly ground black pepper

To serve

6 chicory/Belgian endive leaves

2 fresh red chillies/chiles, deseeded and finely sliced

2 spring onions/scallions, finely sliced

6 cocktail sticks/toothpicks (optional)

Makes 6 sliders

CITY OF LIMERICK PUBLIC LIBRARY

A hearty pork burger with all the traditional breakfast trimmings – for the days when cereal just won't cut it.

big breakfast burger
with a portobello mushroom & a fried egg

For the burgers

2 tablespoons olive oil

5 mushrooms, finely chopped

200 g/7 oz. lean minced/ground pork

2 teaspoons tomato ketchup, homemade (page 61) or store bought

a pinch of mustard powder

3 tablespoons fresh breadcrumbs

a pinch of sea salt and freshly ground black pepper

To serve

2 English muffins

Homemade Tomato Ketchup (page 61)

2 fried eggs

2 grilled/broiled Portobello mushrooms

Makes 2 burgers

Heat 1 tablespoon of the oil in a frying pan/skillet set over medium heat. Add the chopped mushrooms and fry until soft and brown. Remove from the heat and set aside.

Put the pork in a bowl with the tomato ketchup, mustard powder, breadcrumbs and salt and pepper. Work together with your hands until evenly mixed. Add the cooled mushrooms and mix again. Divide the mixture in half and shape into two burger patties. Press each burger down to make them nice and flat.

Heat the remaining oil in the same frying pan and fry the burgers over medium–high heat for 5 minutes on each side until cooked through.

Slice the English muffins in half and lightly toast them under the grill/broiler or in the toaster. Spread a spoonful of Homemade Tomato Ketchup on the base of each muffin and put the cooked burgers on top. Put a fried egg and a grilled/broiled Portobello mushroom on top of each burger and finish with the lids of the English muffins. Serve with extra Homemade Tomato Ketchup on the side.

more meat

This sumptuous pork burger was very popular with our customers when we first started our business. The sweetness of the cider combined with the blue cheese adds a real depth of flavour to this dish. It is even more delicious served with our creamy homemade Classic Mayo.

pork & cider burger
with blue cheese & asparagus

Heat the butter in a frying pan/skillet or stovetop griddle/grill pan set over high heat. Put the asparagus cut-side down in the pan and cook for a couple of minutes. Turn over and brown the other side. Remove from the pan and set aside.

Put the pork in a bowl with the blue cheese, cider, tomato purée/paste and salt and pepper. Work together with your hands until evenly mixed. Divide the mixture in half and shape into two burger patties. Press each burger down to make them nice and flat.

Heat the oil in the same frying pan and fry the burgers over medium–high heat for 5 minutes on each side until cooked through.

Cut the bread rolls in half. Spread a spoonful of Classic Mayo on the bottom half of each roll and put the cooked burgers on top. Lay half the asparagus spears over the top of each burger. Finish with the lids of the bread rolls and serve.

For the burgers

15 g/1 tablespoon butter

6 asparagus spears, sliced down the middle

190 g/6½ oz. lean minced/ground pork

30 g/1½ tablespoons crumbled firm blue cheese (such as Roquefort, Gorgonzola or Stilton)

3 tablespoons (hard) cider

4 teaspoons tomato purée/paste

1 tablespoon olive or vegetable oil

a pinch of sea salt and freshly ground black pepper

To serve

2 seeded wholemeal/wholewheat bread rolls

Classic Mayo (page 58)

Makes 2 burgers

This light Mediterranean-style burger brings you all the flavours of an Italian antipasti spread with every mouthful. These are at their most delicious served in warmed rosemary foccacia rolls.

pork & antipasti burger
with lemon mayo

For the burgers

½ red or yellow (bell) pepper, deseeded and diced

4 mushrooms, diced

70 g/⅔ cup diced aubergine/eggplant

80 g/¾ cup diced courgette/zucchini

2 tablespoons olive oil

140 g/5 oz. lean minced/ground pork

3 tablespoons fresh breadcrumbs

2 teaspoons tomato purée/paste

2 teaspoons fresh green or red pesto

1 garlic clove, crushed

a pinch of sea salt and freshly ground black pepper

To serve

2 rosemary foccacia rolls, warmed

Lemon Mayo (page 59)

a handful of lettuce leaves

lemon wedges, for squeezing

Makes 2 burgers

Preheat the oven to 180°C (350°F) Gas 4.

Put the pepper, mushrooms, aubergine/eggplant and courgette/zucchini in a baking dish with the olive oil and salt and pepper. Roast in the oven for 25–30 minutes until soft and brown. Remove from the oven and set aside to cool. Leave the oven on.

Put the pork in a bowl with the breadcrumbs, tomato purée/paste, pesto, garlic and salt and pepper. Work together with your hands until evenly mixed. Add the cooled vegetables and mix again. Divide the mixture in half and shape into two burger patties. Press each burger down to make them nice and flat. Lay the burgers on a baking sheet and bake in the preheated oven for 25 minutes, turning halfway through cooking.

Cut the rosemary foccacia rolls in half and lightly toast under the grill/broiler or in the toaster. Spread a spoonful of Lemon Mayo on the base of each roll, add the lettuce leaves and top with the cooked burgers. Finish with the lids of the rosemary foccacia rolls and serve with lemon wedges for squeezing.

This Greek-style burger is so tasty and very easy to prepare, making it perfect for a family dinner on a warm evening. The homemade tzatziki adds a delicious touch of authenticity to this dish.

lamb & feta burger
with tzatziki & baby spinach

To make the tzatziki, put the yogurt in a bowl with the cucumber. Add the garlic, olive oil, vinegar, mint and salt, to taste. Mix well with a fork. Cover with clingfilm/plastic wrap and leave to chill in the fridge.

Preheat the grill/broiler to medium–hot.

To make the burgers, put the lamb in a bowl with the feta, onion, olives, garlic, breadcrumbs, cumin, tomato purée/paste and salt and pepper. Work together with your hands until evenly mixed. Divide the mixture in half and shape into two burger patties. Press each burger down to make them nice and flat.

Lay the burgers on a baking sheet and grill/broil for 5 minutes on each side until cooked through.

Cut each of the pittas down one side, to make an opening. Heat a ridged stovetop griddle/grill pan to hot. Put the pittas face down in the pan and turn over after a about 30 seconds to brown the other side. Alternatively, toast lightly in the toaster, taking care not to let them fully toast and crack.

Spread some tzatziki inside each of the warm pittas. Put the cooked burgers inside with a few baby spinach leaves and serve with a spoonful of grated beetroot/beets and baby spinach leaves on the side, if liked.

For the tzatziki

200 g/¾ cup plain yogurt

12-cm/5-inch piece of cucumber, peeled and coarsely grated

1 garlic clove, crushed

1 tablespoon extra virgin olive oil

½ teaspoon red wine vinegar

1 tablespoon finely chopped fresh mint

sea salt

For the burgers

180 g/6 oz. lean minced/ground lamb

30 g/¼ cup chopped feta

½ finely chopped red onion

4 pitted black olives, chopped

1 garlic clove, finely chopped

3 tablespoons fresh breadcrumbs

a pinch of ground cumin

2 teaspoons tomato pureé/paste

a pinch of sea salt and freshly ground black pepper

To serve

2 pitta breads

a handful of baby spinach leaves

2 cooked beetroot/beets, grated

Makes 2 burgers

These tasty little pork bites are oozing with delicious caramelized apple slices. They are always a popular choice with children and so easy! If you have any little ones around you can ask them to help you make them.

pork & apple sliders
with caramelized apple slices

For the sliders

1 Bramley, or other tart apple, peeled and grated

2 tablespoons clear honey

200 g/7 oz. lean minced/ground pork

1 tablespoon olive or vegetable oil

a pinch of sea salt

For the caramelized apple slices

1 tablespoon butter

1 Bramley, or other tart apple, sliced

1 tablespoon brown sugar

To serve

4 mini wholemeal/wholewheat bread rolls

a handful of rocket/arugula leaves

Homemade Tomato Ketchup (page 61)

Makes 4 sliders

Preheat the oven to 180°C (350°F) Gas 4.

To make the sliders, lay the grated apple on a baking sheet and drizzle the honey over the top. Mix well to coat, then bake in the oven for 20–25 minutes until brown and soft, stirring once or twice during cooking. Remove from the oven and set aside to cool.

Put the pork in a bowl with the salt and add the cooled apple. Work together with your hands until evenly mixed. Divide the mixture into quarters and shape into four slider patties. Press each slider down to make them nice and flat. Chill in the fridge while you make the caramelized apple slices.

To make the caramelized apple slices, heat the butter in a frying pan/skillet set over medium-high heat until bubbling. Add the apple slices and cook until tender, crisp and beginning to brown, turning the slices in the pan to brown evenly. Add the sugar and cook until melted and starting to caramelize. Remove from the heat and set aside to cool slightly.

Heat the oil in a frying pan and fry the sliders over medium–high heat for 4 minutes on each side until cooked through.

Slice the mini bread rolls in half and put a few rocket/arugula leaves on the bottom of each. Add the cooked sliders and top each with a slice of caramelized apple. Finish the sliders with the lids of the rolls and serve with Homemade Tomato Ketchup, if liked.

Create a roast-lamb dinner in miniature form with these gourmet sliders. They taste great in a bun, but even better served inside two roast potato rounds.

lamb & mint sliders
with roast potatoes & watercress

Preheat the oven to 180°C (350°F) Gas 4.

Sprinkle 1 tablespoon of the oil on a baking sheet and lay the potato slices on top, mix to coat and sprinkle with black pepper. Bake in the oven for 25 minutes until brown and crisp. Remove from the oven and set aside until cool enough to handle.

Put the lamb in a bowl with the mint, breadcrumbs, egg and salt and pepper. Work together with your hands until evenly mixed. Divide the mixture into quarters and shape into four slider patties. Press each slider down to make them nice and flat.

Heat the remaining oil in a frying pan/skillet and fry the sliders over medium–high heat for 4 minutes on each side until cooked through.

Put one potato round on each serving plate and put a cooked slider on top of each. Top with a few leaves of watercress and finish with another potato round. Put a cocktail stick/toothpick through the middle of each slider to hold them together and serve.

For the sliders

3 tablespoons olive oil

8 roughly-equal rounds of potato, unpeeled

200 g/7 oz. lean minced/ground lamb

6 fresh mint leaves, finely chopped

3 tablespoons fresh breadcrumbs

1 tablespoon beaten egg

a pinch of sea salt and freshly ground black pepper

To serve

a handful of watercress

4 cocktail sticks/toothpicks

Makes 4 sliders

more meat 45

*These deliciously spiced Indian-style sliders pack a good punch.
Served on mini naan breads, they look great and are perfect
canapés for a party or appetizers for an Indian-style feast.*

Indian-style lamb sliders
with minted yogurt & mango chutney

For the sliders

200 g/7 oz. lean minced/
ground lamb

1 tablespoon garam masala

a pinch of ground turmeric

3 tablespoons fresh breadcrumbs

1 tablespoon beaten egg

a pinch of chopped
freshcoriander/cilantro

a pinch of sea salt and freshly
ground black pepper

To serve

4 mini naan breads

plain yogurt mixed with freshly
chopped mint leaves

mango chutney

cocktail sticks/toothpicks (optional)

Makes 4 sliders

Put the lamb in a bowl with the garam masala, turmeric,
breadcrumbs, egg, coriander/cilantro and salt and pepper. Divide
the mixture into quarters and shape into four slider patties. Press
each slider down to make them nice and flat.

Heat the oil in a frying pan/skillet and fry the sliders over medium–
high heat for 4 minutes on each side until cooked through.

Splash a little water on each of the mini naan breads and toast under
the grill/broiler or in a toaster to warm. Put a generous spoonful of
minted yogurt over the top of each mini naan. Top with a cooked
slider and finish with a spoonful of mango chutney. Put a cocktail
stick/toothpick through the middle of each, if needed, and serve.

*This fish pie in burger form is a real treat for anyone who enjoys
a burger but doesn't want to eat meat. Serve with our Classic
Homecut Fries for a hearty and sustaining meal.*

fish pie burger
with capers & tartare sauce

For the burgers

250 g/9 oz. boned salmon fillets

50 g/2 oz. cooked small prawns/
shrimp

30 g/⅓ cup fresh breadcrumbs

1 tablespoon beaten egg

1 tablespoon capers, chopped

1 garlic clove, finely chopped

1 teaspoon finely grated Parmesan
cheese

a good pinch of freshly chopped
chives

a good pinch of freshly chopped
parsley

a pinch of sea salt and freshly
ground black pepper

To serve

2 sesame or plain bagels

tartare sauce

a handful of baby spinach leaves

Classic Homecut Fries (page 57)

Makes 2 large burgers

Preheat the oven to 180°C (350°F) Gas 4.

Put the salmon fillets in a greased baking dish and bake for 20 minutes, turning halfway through cooking. Remove from the oven and set aside until cool enough to handle. Leave the oven on.

Put the prawns/shrimp in a bowl with the breadcrumbs, egg, capers, garlic, Parmesan, chives, parsley and salt and pepper. Work together with your hands until evenly mixed. Remove the skin from the salmon and break it up into flakes, add to the bowl and mix again. Divide the mixture in half and shape into two burger patties. Press each burger down to make them nice and flat.

Lay the burgers on a baking sheet and bake in the preheated oven for 15–20 minutes, turning halfway through cooking.

Slice each bagel in half and lightly toast them under the grill/broiler or in the toaster. Spread the bottom half of each bagel with tartare sauce. Put a cooked burger on top and cover with a few baby spinach leaves. Finish the burgers with the lids of the bagels and serve with Classic Homecut Fries.

other ideas

*These hearty vegetarian burgers don't require a bun because
they are packed full of yummy root vegetables. Serve with our
Mustard Mayo and a mixed leaf salad.*

cheesy root vegetable burger
with mustard mayo

Bring a large saucepan of water to the boil. Put the squash, sweet potato, potato, carrot, onion and garlic and boil for about 10 minutes until soft. Strain and mash well with a potato masher. Add the thyme and salt and pepper and work together with your hands until evenly mixed.

Divide the mixture in half and shape into two burger patties. Press each burger down to make them nice and flat and roll each one in the cheese, so that it sticks all around the outside of the burger.

Preheat the grill/broiler to medium–hot.

Put the burgers on a greased baking sheet and and grill/broil for 6–8 minutes on each side until the cheese is brown and bubbling. Remove from the oven and let cool slightly before serving.

Serve with Mustard Mayo and a mixed leaf salad, if liked.

For the burgers

⅓ butternut squash, peeled and chopped

1 sweet potato, peeled and chopped

1 small potato, peeled and chopped

1 carrot, peeled and chopped

½ red onion, chopped

1 garlic clove, chopped

a large pinch of dried thyme

40 g/⅓ cup grated mature/sharp Cheddar cheese

a pinch of sea salt and freshly ground black pepper

To serve (optional)

Mustard Mayo (page 58)

a mixed leaf salad

Makes 2 burgers

These cute sliders combine all the ingredients of a chicken Caesar salad. They're light and delicious and make great canapés to serve at parties – perfect for entertaining.

chicken Caesar sliders
wrapped in Parma ham with Caesar dressing

For the Caesar dressing

1 egg yolk

1 small garlic clove, crushed

2 anchovy fillets in oil, drained and chopped

1 tablespoon freshly squeezed lemon juice

1 teaspoon Worcestershire sauce

150 ml/⅔ cup olive oil

25 g/1 oz. Parmesan cheese, finely grated

sea salt and freshly ground black pepper

For the sliders

200 g/7 oz. lean minced/ ground chicken or turkey

6 chives, finely chopped

1 teaspoon anchovy paste

20 g/¾ oz. Parmesan cheese, finely grated

1 teaspoon beaten egg

a pinch of sea salt and freshly ground black pepper

2 slices Parma ham, cut in half

To serve

4 seeded mini rolls

a handful of Romano lettuce leaves

4 cocktail sticks/toothpicks

Makes 4 sliders

Preheat the oven to 180°C (350°F) Gas 4.

To make the Caesar dressing, whisk the egg yolk in a small bowl with the garlic, anchovies, lemon juice, Worcestershire sauce and salt and pepper, to taste, until frothy. Gradually whisk in the olive oil a little at a time until thick and glossy. Add 2 tablespoons of water to thin the dressing and stir in the Parmesan. Store in a screw-top jar in the fridge and use the same day.

To make the sliders, put the chicken in a bowl with the chives, anchovy paste, Parmesan, egg and salt and pepper. Work together with your hands until evenly mixed. Divide the mixture into quarters and shape into four slider patties. Press each slider down to make them nice and flat.

Wrap a piece of Parma ham around each slider and lay them on a baking sheet. Bake the sliders in the preheated oven for 15–20 minutes until cooked through.

Cut each of the rolls in half and put a Romano lettuce leaf on the bottom half of each roll. Top each with a cooked slider, drizzle with Caesar dressing and finish with the lids of the rolls. Put a cocktail stick/toothpick through the middle of each slider to hold it in place and serve.

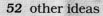

These seasonal sliders are perfect served as festive canapés or appetizers for a winter menu. They are also great for using up any leftovers you may have during the holiday season.

Christmas canapé sliders
with cranberry sauce & camembert

Preheat the oven to 180°C (350°F) Gas 4.

Put the parsnip in a baking dish, drizzle with the honey and toss to coat. Bake in the oven for 25–30 minutes until soft and starting to brown. Remove from the oven and leave to cool.

Put the turkey in a bowl with the egg, tomato purée/paste, chestnuts, breadcrumbs and salt and pepper. Divide the mixture into five equal pieces and shape into five slider patties. Press each slider down to make them nice and flat.

Heat the oil in a frying pan/skillet and fry the sliders over medium–high heat for 4 minutes on each side until cooked through.

Put the sliders on a serving plate and cover each with a square of Camembert. Top the sliders with a slice of roasted parsnip and put a cocktail stick/toothpick through the middle of each slider to hold them in place. Serve with a bowl of cranberry sauce for spooning.

For the sliders

1 parsnip, cut into 1-cm/¾-inch slices

1 tablespoon runny honey

160 g/5½ oz. lean minced/ground turkey

1 tablespoon beaten egg

2 teaspoons tomato purée/paste

3 cooked chestnuts, finely chopped

3 tablespoons fresh breadcrumbs

1 tablespoon olive or vegetable oil

sea salt and freshly ground black pepper

To serve

5 squares of Camembert cheese

cranberry sauce

5 cocktail sticks/toothpicks

Makes 5 sliders

homemade fries

sweet potato fries

2 sweet potatoes, skin on, sliced into wedges

olive oil for drizzling

sea salt and freshly ground black pepper

cajun spice rub (optional)

Serves 2

Preheat the oven to 180°C (350°F) Gas 4.

Bring a large saucepan of water to the boil. Add the sweet potatoes and boil for about 5 minutes. Remove from the pan and lay on a greased baking sheet.

Drizzle some olive oil over the top, sprinkle with black pepper and cajun spice rub, if using and mix to coat.

Bake in the oven for 25 minutes until brown and crisp. Shake the baking sheet frequently to make sure the fries brown evenly without sticking.

Remove from the oven, sprinkle with salt and serve immediately.

sauces & sides

classic homecut fries

2 floury potatoes, sliced
into fries
olive oil for drizzling
sea salt and freshly ground
black pepper

Serves 2

Preheat the oven to 180°C (350°F)
Gas 4.

Bring a large saucepan of water to
the boil. Add the potatoes and
boil for about 5 minutes. Remove
from the pan and lay on a greased
baking sheet.

Drizzle some olive oil over the
top, sprinkle with salt and pepper,
to taste, and mix to coat. Bake in
the oven for 25 minutes until
brown and crisp.

Shake the baking sheet frequently
to make sure the fries brown
evenly without sticking.

Remove from the oven, sprinkle
with salt and serve immediately.

mayos

Homemade mayonnaise is far more tasty than store-bought versions and using a food processor means it's so simple to make.

classic mayo

3 egg yolks
2 teaspoons Dijon mustard
2 teaspoons white wine vinegar
or freshly squeezed lemon juice
½ teaspoon sea salt
300 ml/1¼ cups olive oil

Makes about 400 ml/1¾ cups

Put the egg yolks, mustard, vinegar or lemon juice and salt in a food processor and blend until foaming. With the blade running, gradually pour in the oil through a funnel until thick and glossy. If it is too thick add a little water . Taste and adjust the seasoning, if necessary.

Spoon into a bowl and serve. Keep in the fridge for up to three days.

mustard mayo

1 recipe Classic Mayo
2 tablespoons wholegrain mustard

Makes about 400 ml/1¾ cups

Make the Classic Mayo following the method in the recipe, left, but omitting the Dijon mustard. Transfer to a bowl and stir in the wholegrain mustard. Use as required or store as before.

herb mayo

1 recipe Classic Mayo

a handful of any fresh green
herbs, such as basil, parsley or
tarragon, chopped

Makes about 400 ml/1¾ cups

Make the Classic Mayo following
the method in the recipe, far left.
Add the herbs to the food processor
and blend until the sauce is speckled
green. Use as required or store as
before.

lemon mayo

1 recipe Classic Mayo

1 teaspoon freshly squeezed
lemon juice

1 teaspoon finely grated lemon zest

a pinch of freshly ground
black pepper

Makes about 400 ml/1¾ cups

Make the Classic Mayo following
the method in the recipe, far left,
adding the lemon juice, zest and
pepper with the mustard and
vinegar. Blend until thickened.
Use as required or store as before.

* Variation: For a Lime Mayo, simply
replace the lemon zest and juice with
the zest and juice from a lime.

pesto mayo

1 recipe Classic Mayo

1 teaspoon fresh green pesto

Makes about 400 ml/1¾ cups

Make the Classic Mayo following the
method in the recipe, far left, adding
the pesto at the same time as the
mustard and vinegar. Blend until
thickened. Use as required or store
as before.

sauces

*Homemade sauces taste fantastic.
They are simple to make and will store
well for up to 5 days or for several weeks
in sterilized jars stored in the fridge.*

hot & smoky barbecue sauce

200 ml/¾ cup passata/
Italian sieved tomatoes

100 ml/scant ½ cup maple
syrup

50 ml/3 tablespoons black
treacle/dark molasses

50 ml/3 tablespoons tomato
ketchup, homemade (see recipe
right) or store bought

50 ml/3 tablespoons white
wine vinegar

2 tablespoons Worcestershire
sauce

1 tablespoon hot chilli/
chili sauce

2 teaspoons Dijon mustard

1 teaspoon garlic powder

1 teaspoon smoked paprika

sea salt and freshly ground
black pepper

Makes 350 ml/1½ cups

Put all the ingredients in a
saucepan, bring to the boil and
simmer gently for 15 minutes
until thickened and reduced.
Season to taste with salt and
pepper, then let cool completely.
Pour into a clean jar and store in
the fridge for up to five days. If
using sterilized jars, pour the hot
sauce directly into the jar and
when cold, seal and store in the
fridge. It will keep for a few weeks.

homemade tomato ketchup

2 tablespoons olive oil

1 onion, finely chopped

2 garlic cloves, crushed

450 ml/2 scant cups tomato passata/Italian sieved tomatoes

150 ml/⅔ cup red wine vinegar

150 g/¾ cup soft brown sugar

2 tablespoons black treacle/dark molasses

2 tablespoons tomato purée/paste

1 teaspoon Dijon mustard

2 bay leaves

1 teaspoon sea salt

½ teaspoon freshly ground black pepper

Makes about 400 ml/1¾ cups

Heat the oil in a saucepan, add the onion and garlic and fry gently for 10 minutes until softened.

Add all the remaining ingredients, bring to the boil, reduce the heat and simmer gently for 30 minutes until thickened and reduced by about one third.

Pass the sauce through a sieve/strainer, let cool and pour into a clean bottle and store in the fridge for up to five days. If using sterilized bottles, pour the hot sauce directly into the bottle and when cold, seal and store in the fridge. It will keep for a few weeks.

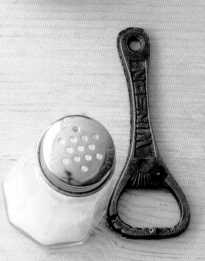

coleslaws

classic coleslaw

125 g/1 generous cup shredded
white cabbage

125 g/1 generous cup shredded
red cabbage

175 g/1½ cups grated carrots

½ white onion, thinly sliced

1 teaspoon sea salt, plus extra
for seasoning

2 teaspoons caster sugar

1 tablespoon white wine vinegar

50 ml/3½ tablespoons Classic Mayo
(page 58)

50 g/3 tablespoons single/light cream

freshly ground black pepper

Makes 500 g/2 cups

Put the white and red cabbage, carrots and
onion in a colander and sprinkle with the salt,
sugar and vinegar. Stir well and let drain over
a bowl for 20 minutes.

Transfer the vegetables to a clean tea towel
and squeeze out any excess liquid. Put them
in a large bowl and stir in the mayo and
cream. Season to taste with salt and pepper
and serve.

sour cream slaw

1 celery stalk, grated
80 g/⅔ cup grated green cabbage
1 carrot, peeled and grated
½ red onion (or 3 spring
onions/scallions), finely chopped
1 teaspoon wholegrain mustard
1 tablespoon white wine vinegar
1 teaspoon dark brown sugar
100 ml/scant ½ cup sour cream
sea salt and freshly ground black
pepper

Makes 500 g/2 cups

Put the celery, cabbage, carrot and onion in a large bowl. Stir in the mustard, white wine vinegar, sugar and sour cream. Season to taste with salt and pepper and serve.

index